LINCOLNSHIRE
The Glorious County

PETER AND JANET ROWORTH

HALSGROVE

First published in Great Britain in 2015

British Library Cataloguing-in-Publication Data
A CIP record for this title is available from the British Library

ISBN 978 0 85704 275 0

HALSGROVE
Halsgrove House,
Ryelands Business Park,
Bagley Road, Wellington, Somerset TA21 9PZ
Tel: 01823 653777   Fax: 01823 216796
email: sales@halsgrove.com

Part of the Halsgrove group of companies
Information on all Halsgrove titles is available at:
www.halsgrove.com

Printed in China by Everbest Printing Co Ltd

Contents

Introduction and Acknowledgements

LINCOLNSHIRE IS OUR COUNTY; we love the range of unspoilt landscapes and the wonderful feeling of space. We are fortunate to live on the coast and have dunes, salt marsh and enormous expanses of sand to enjoy, but we need to cross the Wolds whenever we travel inland, and when we rise up onto the hills it is like being on top of the world. We have a close affinity to the agriculture of the county and take great pleasure in seeing a herd of Lincolnshire Red cattle grazing or watching a large and colourful tractor ploughing the land, hopefully accompanied by a host of seagulls. We enjoy the progression of the seasons and the effect this has on the landscape; watching the fields and hedgerows change colour throughout the year. We like to explore the rich heritage of the county, visiting houses, churches and museums in the towns and villages. And whenever we approach Lincoln we look out for the Cathedral, visible on the skyline; there is surely no other cathedral in the country that has such a magnificent setting.

The photographs are our own but we acknowledge the help of various sources in the preparation of the text, particularly the Lincolnshire volume of *The Buildings of England* by Nikolaus Pevsner and John Harris, revised by Nicholas Antram, and *An Historical Atlas of Lincolnshire* edited by Stewart Bennett and Nicholas Bennett. We have used many internet sources, particularly lincoln.gov.uk, lincolnshire.gov.uk, thelincolnite.co.uk, visitlincoln.com, and lincoln.ac.uk. We have followed the divisions of the county that were adopted by Lincolnshire Tourism, and the map of the same is reproduced courtesy of Lincolnshire County Council. We acknowledge the permission of Holiday Inn Express, Lincoln to photograph from the roof, Hemswell Antiques Centres to photograph inside The Guardroom, and Jack Buck Farms to photograph daffodils in their fields. Thanks are due to Neil Wright who provided additional information on Boston.

Peter and Janet Roworth

Map of Lincolnshire

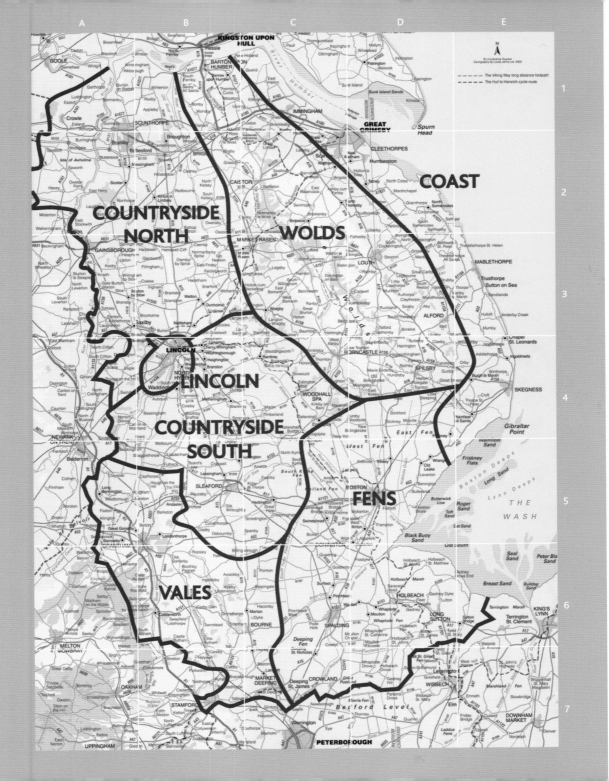

Lincoln

LINCOLN IS SITED where a gap in the limestone cliff allows the River Witham to flow through and so out to the sea at Boston. The Romans recognised the strategic importance of the site and founded a legionary fortress on the level ground on top of the northern slope; traces of the walls and the northern gate still survive. But an earlier Iron Age community already existed on the banks of the Brayford Pool. The north-south limestone ridge provided a natural routeway that became the Roman Ermine Way and further development of the town spread southwards down the slope to the river where there was a crossing point. The Romans were also responsible for the Foss Dyke, a canal that connects the Witham to the River Trent.

In the centuries after the Roman occupation Lincoln suffered a period of de-population and much of the grid system of roads was lost. However reoccupation and growth began by 900 and many of the city's parishes originated in the following century. By 1066 the town was once again flourishing with evidence of some industrial activity and trade along the waterways. William the Conqueror had a castle erected in a dominant position within the old Roman fort; the castle bailey took over the remainder of the fort and this became The Bail, a name that continues in use to this day in Bailgate. Building of the Norman Cathedral began in 1072 and there were further phases of enlargement throughout the medieval period. The Bishop of Lincoln controlled a vast diocese that stretched from the Humber to the Thames, and Lincoln became one of the largest towns outside London, its wealth largely based on the cloth and wool trades.

The city played a part in the Magna Carta story and it still holds one of the four remaining original charters, displayed in a new vault in Lincoln Castle. The city may have declined after the Middle Ages but it remained the cultural capital of the county and many of the gentry families had their town houses where they could come to attend the assizes, the assemblies and balls, and the Lincoln Races.

By the mid nineteenth century the city was undergoing a revival as a commercial centre; the railways arrived and Lincoln became a great centre of heavy engineering, manufacturing steam engines, agricultural implements, threshing machines and excavators. In the twentieth century aeroplanes were built and the tank was developed, all part of the war effort; but in the post-war era there was a steady decline in large-scale engineering in the city, leaving just the production and servicing of gas-turbine engines. But Lincoln has continued to grow and diversify, new housing projects have been undertaken, new retail parks created, and the opening of the university has brought considerable investment and had a major influence on the life of the city.

Opposite: **View of Lincoln and the Cathedral from Canwick; Jews' Court Books sign; The Steep Hill Tea Rooms and Chocolatier sign; The Magna Carta public house sign**

Lucy Tower at Lincoln Castle

Lincoln Castle was first built in 1068, just two years after the Norman Conquest. Lucy Tower was constructed around sixty years later on the original castle mound. In the past it had higher walls and it contained the living quarters for the Constable of the Castle. In the nineteenth century it was used as a burial ground for prisoners who had died or were hanged for their crimes, and the small gravestones can still be seen around the base of the trees that grow within its walls.

Opposite: **Observatory Tower at Lincoln Castle**

The Observatory Tower in the south-east corner of the Castle is partly Norman but it was reconstructed in the early nineteenth century using convict labour from the prison. John Merryweather, the prison governor, was a keen astronomer and he wanted somewhere to observe the stars in the night sky.

Prison and David PJ Ross Magna Carta Vault at Lincoln Castle

Lincoln is proud to possess one of the four remaining copies of Magna Carta issued in 1215 and now housed in a state-of-the-art vault constructed between the Georgian and Victorian prison buildings. Drawn up by the barons and agreed by King John, it was a charter of liberties that would change the course of history. Also on display is Lincoln's copy of the Charter of the Forest issued in 1217 which was concerned with the forest laws that operated over the vast areas of royal forest that were set aside for the king's hunting.

Heritage Skills Centre at Lincoln Castle
This modern building with its grass roof is designed to fit unobtrusively within the Castle grounds. It is a focus for heritage crafts and skills development, providing hands-on experience and training through demonstrations and short courses.

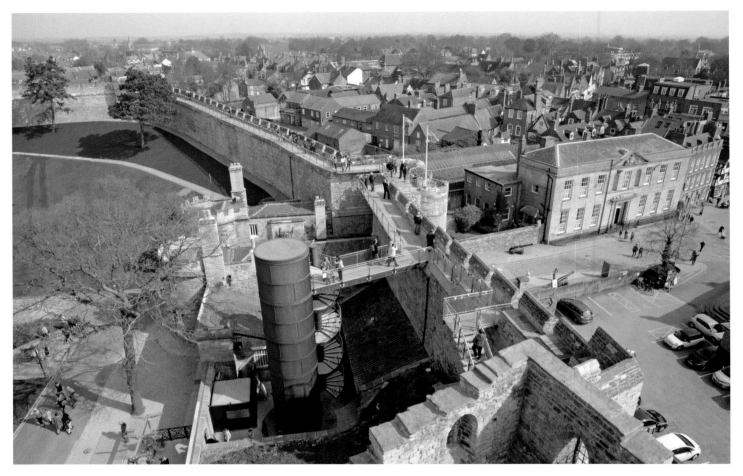

View from the Observatory Tower of the Castle's East Gate and Wall Walk
Visitors to the Castle can access the Medieval Wall Walk by the new lift tower or spiral staircase. They can then walk the full circumference, a distance of a third of a mile, with stunning views over the Castle courtyard and across the city of Lincoln.

Opposite: **View from the Observatory Tower of Castle Hill and the Cathedral**
The two great buildings of Lincoln, the Castle and the Cathedral, both begun by William the Conqueror, face each other across Castle Hill. In the centre is the Judges' Lodging, built to accommodate the judges that visited the city to preside over the Assize Courts; now the magnificent rooms can be hired as a wedding venue.

Opposite: Lincoln Cathedral

The building of the first cathedral was started soon after the Norman Conquest of 1066. However it was during the twelfth to fourteenth centuries that the magnificent building that we see today was constructed. Although some rounded arches remain from the earliest Norman phase of building, most of the architecture is of the Early English Gothic style with pointed arches, ribbed vaults and flying buttresses, which enabled much higher roof spans and the creation of larger windows. The two west towers were heightened around 1370 to 1400, and these and the taller central tower all had spires until 1549, when the latter was blown down. It had been the tallest building in the world.

Right: Castle Hill, Lincoln

This is not a hill but a space that links the Castle and the Cathedral through Exchequer Gate. The largest of the gates in the Cathedral Close wall, Exchequer Gate dates from the fourteenth century and has three arches; it was where tenants who rented property from the church would come to pay their rents, laying their money on a chequered cloth.

Statue of Alfred, Lord Tennyson, Minster Green

Alfred, Lord Tennyson was born in Somersby in Lincolnshire in 1809 and buried in Poets' Corner, Westminster Abbey in 1892, but he is commemorated in the county of his birth by this magnificent statue. Set within the grounds of the Cathedral, the statue was the work of his friend George Frederick Watts who wanted to portray Tennyson's love for nature, and so he is shown pondering over the root and stem of a little flower which he holds in his hand, while a verse from 'Flower in a Crannied Wall' is inscribed on the plinth. Tennyson's dog Karenina is also shown, patiently watching her master.

Opposite: Minster Yard

Beyond the lime trees on Minster Green are these attractive buildings, part of the Cathedral Close. While some are in residential use, others are used by local preparatory schools.

Potter Gate

This is what remains of the fourteenth century gatehouse that helped protect the Cathedral Close. Originally it housed a portcullis, and the guardroom had its own fireplace and garderobe. Until relatively recently traffic passed through the arch but the road is now taken around the gatehouse through a break in the Close wall.

Opposite: **Chapter House**

Built in the early thirteenth century the Chapter House is a ten-sided building whose original purpose was as a meeting place for the Chapter, the canons of the Cathedral. Nowadays it makes a very special place for concerts and for entertaining.

Tourist Information Centre, Castle Hill
The magnificent timber-framed building known as Leigh-Pemberton House has survived from the sixteenth century when it would have been home to a wealthy merchant. From 1899 to 1979 it served the city as a bank, and it was given to the city of Lincoln by Sir Robin Leigh-Pemberton who later became Governor of the Bank of England.

Lincoln Hotel, Eastgate

This very modern building with its 1960s' architecture is set in the heart of uphill Lincoln and it has some of the best views of the Cathedral. In front of the hotel there are the exposed foundations of part of the eastern gateway into the Roman town.

Opposite: **Water tower, Westgate**
Standing just outside the Castle walls this water tower was cleverly disguised to look like the keep. It holds around three million gallons of water, pumped from Elkesley in Nottinghamshire. It was built in 1911 to provide a clean water supply to the residents of the city following a typhoid epidemic in 1905.

Right: **Ellis's Mill, Mill Road**
The brick tower is dated 1798 but a windmill has been on this site from at least the middle of the seventeenth century. It is the last survivor of the nine windmills that once stood on Lincoln Cliff and it has been fully restored and is run by a dedicated band of volunteer millers who produce and sell flour.

Newport Arch

This was the North Gate of the Roman walled city and it is the only Roman gateway in the country which still has traffic flowing through it, although there have been some unfortunate incidents with vehicles that have mis-judged its height and become jammed underneath. A fine section of Roman wall known as the Mint Wall survives nearby in West Bight.

Museum of Lincolnshire Life, Burton Road
Originally the Victorian barracks built for the Royal North Lincoln Militia in 1857, the buildings have now become the home of the Museum of Lincolnshire Life. It is set out with period rooms and old shops; there is a nationally important collection of agricultural machines and the iconic World War One tank that was developed and built by Foster's of Lincoln. The museum also houses the Royal Lincolnshire Regimental Galleries.

Lincolnshire Sausage Festival, Lincoln Castle

Lincolnshire is justly proud of its sausages, made with coarsely chopped pork and seasoned with the herb sage. Each year the people of Lincolnshire celebrate the famous sausage with a festival held in and around the Castle grounds which includes cooking demonstrations, food stalls, children's entertainment and live music.

Opposite: Sausage Festival flag; Sizzling sausages; Folk group entertaining visitors to the Sausage Festival

Bailgate

This is the most important street in the uphill Cathedral Quarter of Lincoln. At one end is Newport Arch and it follows the route of the Roman Ermine Street. The other end of Bailgate leads into Castle Hill. It is noted for its range of specialist shops and places to eat.

Opposite: An unusual view of the Post Office where Bailgate meets Eastgate

Steep Hill
Many of the buildings on Steep Hill have medieval timber-framing but this is often hidden behind later shop fronts.

Cobbled and narrow, this popular tourist street is flying the flags for Lincolnshire Day which is celebrated every year on 1 October, the date marking the anniversary of the Lincolnshire Rising, a revolt against Henry VIII in 1536.

The Jew's House and Jews' Court, Steep Hill

On the left is the two-storey Jew's House, a stone-built house of the later twelfth century which originally had arched openings for shops on the ground floor, with the living accommodation complete with fireplace (over the ornamental doorway) on the floor above. The building to the right is Jews' Court and here the stone front is later, probably seventeenth century. The building may have been the medieval Jewish synagogue, but it now houses the offices and bookshop of the Society for Lincolnshire History and Archaeology.

A mix of shop signs, old and new, on Steep Hill

Harlequin Antiquarian Books, Steep Hill
Once a public house known as the Harlequin Inn this was a regular drinking haunt for the theatre folk from nearby Drury Lane. Now this ancient timber-framed building is an antiquarian and second-hand bookshop. It is picturesquely placed at the junction with Michaelgate and appears to have sunk into the road.

Opposite: **Bandstand in the Arboretum**
The Arboretum was designed by Edward Milner, one of the most celebrated Victorian gardeners of his time, as a public park for the people of the city, and it opened in 1872. It included trees, shrubs and flower borders, lakes, fountains and a maze. The Victorian cast-iron bandstand was restored as part of the renovation work that preceded its re-opening in 2003.

Opposite: **Empowerment sculpture, South Waterside**

This Millennium sculpture by Stephen Broadbent is made of cast aluminium and steel. Inspired by the blades of a gas turbine, the two stylised human figures reach out to empower one another. The sculpture spans the River Witham in front of the Waterside shopping centre.

Right: **Narrowboat approaching High Bridge**

High Bridge takes the High Street over the River Witham. It still carries a row of sixteenth-century shops and houses making it unique in England. Also known as the Glory Hole, boats need to have a maximum height of 2.8m to pass underneath and they can then travel on the Witham Navigation down to the Grand Sluice at Boston. From Brayford Pool boats can also go upstream via the Fossdyke Navigation to Torksey Lock on the River Trent.

The Guildhall and Stonebow, High Street

This has been the site of a gateway since Roman times. The present building was begun in the late fifteenth century but it has been much altered and restored. The Guildhall is on the upper floor, the largest room being the Council Chamber which is still used by the City Council for meetings and events. The carved statues are of the Virgin Mary and the Angel Gabriel, while the royal coat of arms is that of James I who visited the city in 1617. The clock dates from 1888.

Shoppers on the High Street
Lincoln's High Street runs north to south and is home to over 300 shops and restaurants, including many favourite high street names.

Usher Gallery, Lindum Hill

The art gallery was opened in 1927 following a bequest made to the city by the jeweller James Ward Usher. It combines displays from its permanent collection of fine and decorative arts, and horology (clocks and watches), with a programme of temporary exhibitions. Highlights include the eighteenth century portrait of Joseph Banks, Lincoln views by the artist Peter De Wint, and James Ward Usher's collections of watches, miniatures, porcelain and silver.

The Collection, Danes Terrace

The Collection is a new name for a new building opened in 2005, but the museum contents have been amassed over a long period of time and they were once housed in the Greyfriars building on Broadgate. The new purpose-built archaeology gallery at The Collection tells the story of Lincolnshire's rich heritage through displays, reconstructions and hands-on activities.

The University of Lincoln

The building of the main campus of the University of Lincoln on the southern side of Brayford Pool has transformed an area of redundant railway yards and sidings. The University has invested in state-of-the-art research and teaching facilities and formed successful partnerships with many local businesses.

Students at the University of Lincoln

With courses as diverse as performing arts, journalism, psychology, sport and exercise, mathematics and engineering, the University attracts students from across the country and from overseas. The fusion of old and new, ancient and contemporary, makes Lincoln an exciting place for students to live and study.

Green Dragon public house, Waterside North
This four-gabled timber-framed building dates from around 1500 when it was probably the home of a wealthy wool merchant. The building has only been the Green Dragon public house since it was restored and extended in the 1950s, replacing a much smaller pub of the same name that adjoined it on the east side.

Drill Hall sculpture, Free School Lane

Opened in 1890, the Drill Hall was built as a military and police training hall but it was also used for community and social events. After restoration and the creation of a large auditorium and modern café bar, the hall re-opened in 2004 as an entertainment venue hosting theatre, comedy, talks and films as well as live music events. The striking sculpture on the exterior wall is by Rick Kirby, known for his use of welded steel.

The Engine Shed, University of Lincoln
Housed in a renovated railway engine shed, this student centre on the university campus provides the city with a large multi-purpose entertainment venue.

Opposite: **Pleasure Boats moored in Brayford Pool**
Brayford Pool is a natural lake formed from a widening of the River Witham in the centre of the city. In the past it would have been busy with vessels trading all manner of goods and the waterfront was lined with warehouses and hostelries for the crews. Now the pool is used as a marina by houseboats and pleasure craft.

Left: **Central Library,
Free School Lane**
The library building with its domed
centre was designed by Sir Reginald
Blomfield and opened in 1914. It
offers books, DVDs, and CDs for
loan, provides computers for online
resources, holds a wealth of
information on local history, and it is
home to the Tennyson Research
Centre, the most significant collection
of material on Alfred Tennyson in the
world.

Opposite: **The Obelisk,
St Mark's Shopping Centre**
The shops in the St Mark's complex
have been built on the site of the old
Midland Railway station yard. The
Obelisk was originally positioned on
the east side of High Bridge and it
served as a water conduit where the
people of Lincoln could collect their
drinking water. It was removed from
the bridge in 1939 and recreated here
in 1996.

**View looking east from the rooftop of the
Holiday Inn Express, Ruston Way**
The University buildings are on the left and with St Mark's Retail
Park on the right.

Left: **View looking north-east from the rooftop of
the Holiday Inn Express, Ruston Way**
In the foreground there is the modern architecture of the University
of Lincoln buildings, but it is the magnificent Cathedral that
dominates the city.

Footbridge over Broadgate
Broadgate is the main north-south through route for traffic in Lincoln so the footbridge at Waterside South is a welcome means of crossing this busy road. It also provides walkers with a superb view of Lincoln Cathedral on the cliff above.

View of Lincoln Cathedral from Broadgate

Opposite: **Central Station, St Mary's Street**
The baronial-style building was completed in 1848 for the Great Northern Railway. It is now managed by East Midland Trains with services to Newark, Sheffield, Peterborough and Grimsby.

The Lincolnshire Co-op Stand at Lincoln City football stadium
The Lincoln City football club have played at Sincil Bank, known to fans as 'The Bank', since 1895. They are nicknamed 'The Imps' after the legend of the Lincoln Imp, a stone carving high up on a pillar in the Angel Choir of Lincoln Cathedral which has been adopted as a symbol for Lincoln.

Inset: **The Lincoln Imp, on the gate of the Usher Gallery**

Cornhill Market

Lincoln's Cornhill Market is open every day and it has a variety of stalls to tempt shoppers to come inside. There are also regular Farmers' Markets held on City Square, the High Street and Castle Hill which showcase the best produce that the county has to offer.

Railway crossing, Brayford Wharf East
A train whizzes past on the level crossing as students wait to cross.

Christmas shoppers, High Street
There is something special about Christmas shopping as daylight fades and the lights come on overhead.

Christmas Market, Castle Hill
Held each year in early December, Lincoln's Christmas Market has become one of the most popular in Europe. The idea for a Christmas market was adopted from Lincoln's twin town of Neustadt an der Weinstrasse in Germany. The market stalls are spread around the Castle and Cathedral in this historic part of the city.

Opposite: **Christmas Market, Bishops' Palace**
The floodlit Cathedral makes a wonderful backdrop to the market stalls selling gifts and food to the many visitors.

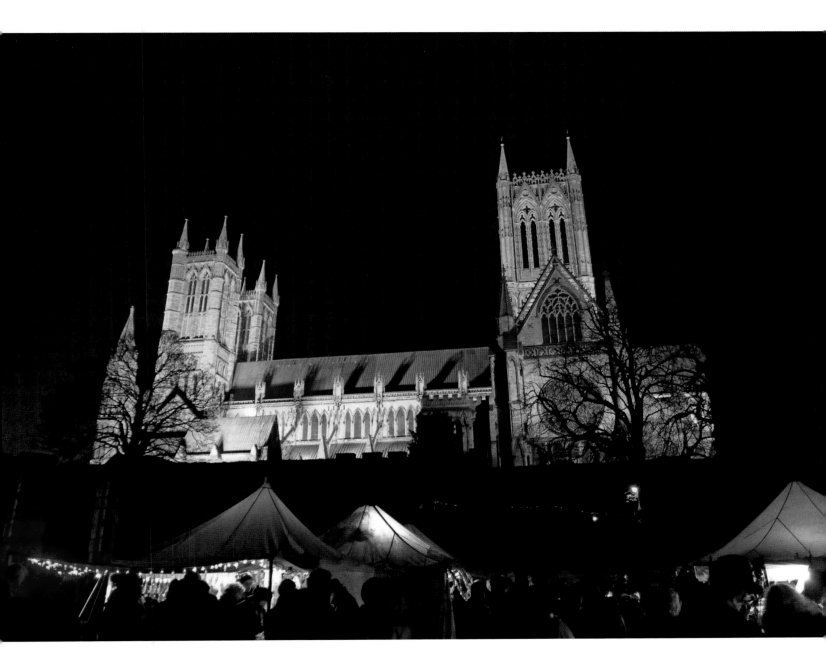

Lincoln Big Ice Rink, City Square

Skaters brave the cold and enjoy the real ice that appears every year in the lead up to Christmas. It is a great place to combine exercise and fun. This image captures the slow and sedate beginners, the reasonably confident, and those going so fast you can barely see them as they fly by in a blur.

Christmas Market, Westgate
The big wheel and carousel are part of the funfair that accompanies the Christmas Market.

View of strip fields in the Isle of Axholme

Countryside North

THIS AREA TO THE NORTH of Lincoln has a central spine of high ground along the limestone cliff with low-lying river valleys on both sides; to the west is the Trent Vale and to the east is the River Ancholme. The old Roman road known as the Ermine Way runs up the centre of the higher ground, and nowadays this route is mainly under the A15. A possibly even older route known as Middle Street and now the B1398 runs to the west of the A15 and provides wonderful views over the Trent Vale. Towards the northern end of the limestone ridge is the town of Scunthorpe which developed spectacularly in the nineteenth century when the local ironstone was mined. For much of its length the River Trent forms the county boundary between Lincolnshire and Nottinghamshire. Gainsborough developed as an important port on the river and here the first bridge crossing was constructed in 1790. North of Gainsborough and separated from the rest of the county by the River Trent is the Isle of Axholme. It is hard to visualise this area as an island but before the extensive drainage that began with the work of Cornelius Vermuyden in the seventeenth century, the settlements like Crowle and Epworth stood on the high ground surrounded by bog and marsh. Although small areas of the bog remain and are now protected as nature reserves, most of this low-lying ground has been turned into productive farmland, while parts of the higher ground have some unique surviving fragments of the strip farming system that was once widespread. The valley of the River Ancholme was also an area that was subject to flooding until the river was straightened which gave the dual benefit of draining the farmland and bringing trade to the town of Brigg. The old name of Glandford Bridge shows that Brigg grew up on the crossing point of the River Ancholme.

Statue of John Wesley, Epworth; Sign for The Guardroom, Hemswell Antique Centres; The Old Hall, Gainsborough

Riseholme Hall

The hall was built for the Chaplin family in the mid eighteenth century, but was remodelled a century later when it became the Palace for the Bishop of Lincoln. By the early twentieth century the hall with its farms and parkland had been acquired by the County Council for the purpose of establishing a farm institute. For much of the last century the hall was the centrepiece of a thriving agricultural college, with students residing in hostels built in the grounds. It remains a unique green space within walking distance of the city of Lincoln.

Julian's Bower and Alkborough Flats

The turf maze, known as Julian's Bower, is of ancient origin and was first recorded back in 1697. It overlooks the confluence of the Rivers Trent and Ouse (Humber) and Alkborough Flats, an area of former farmland which has become a site of managed coastal realignment. Here the outer defences have been breached so that water enters the site at high tide. The various lagoons have become an attractive habitat for breeding and wintering wildfowl and wading birds.

The Old Hall, Gainsborough

This is one of the best preserved medieval manor houses in the country, with a stunning timber-framed great hall, east and west ranges of lodging rooms, and a brick tower, all built in the fifteenth century. The brick kitchen range is a wonderful survival, much used in film and television work because of the enormous fireplaces and bread ovens.

Doddington Hall

The hall is a fine example of late Elizabethan architecture, having been built at the end of the sixteenth century. After 400 years of unbroken family occupation it houses a wonderful collection of furniture, weaponry, paintings, ceramics and textiles, and it is open to the public during the summer months. There are also extensive gardens and nearby a superb farm shop, café and restaurant.

Inside The Guardroom, Hemswell Antique Centres

The buildings that form the Hemswell Antique Centres were once part of RAF Hemswell, one of the Second World War bomber bases in the county, but they are now stuffed full of antiques and collectables from bygone times. There are dealers selling furniture, porcelain, pottery and glass, clocks, silverware, paintings – the list goes on and on.

Marshall's Yard, Gainsborough

Historic buildings which once formed part of Marshall's Britannia Iron Works, have been transformed into a unique retail environment. Where once steam engines and threshing machines were built, there are now shops and restaurants in a courtyard setting, the new architecture blending sensitively with the old.

Wrawby Street, Brigg

Leading from the Market Place this is the main shopping street, but Brigg is also famous for its 'courts'; little yards that open off the main street and are home to many niche enterprises. The annual Horse Fair, organised by the travelling community, still takes place in August, and attracts many hundreds of spectators who come to see the horses being paraded through the town.

Old River Ancholme, Brigg

The Old River Ancholme flows through the town of Brigg and there is a marina and mooring for cabin cruisers and narrowboats. A towpath follows the river, which is also used by rowing and canoe clubs. The New River Ancholme has been canalized and it carries most of the water that drains from the surrounding farmland in the Vale of Ancholme.

Tractors ploughing at The Festival of the Plough
The Festival, held each year in September, offers visitors the chance to see shire horses and old tractors ploughing the land, while the exhibitors compete against each other for prizes. There are displays of vintage machinery and vehicles, entertainments and food, ensuring that families have a great day out, while also raising money for charity.

Opposite: **Tractor ploughing on The Levels**
Once subject to annual flooding, the flat land of the Isle of Axholme is rich fertile farmland, used to grow crops of wheat and potatoes.

The Old Rectory, Epworth

This impressive building was completed in 1709 for Samuel Wesley, Rector of Epworth after the original rectory had burnt down. Samuel and his wife Susannah had ten children including John and Charles who went on to develop the Methodist movement. The building is now a museum and is open to the public.

Opposite: **Dirtness Pumping Station, Belton**

The flat land of the Isle of Axholme is criss-crossed with many drainage channels like the North Engine Drain shown here. Windmills would have originally been used to pump water from these channels, replaced in the nineteenth century by more efficient steam pumps. Time has moved on and now the pumps are electric, but the fine Victorian buildings survive.

Tractor and drill working near Binbrook

Right: Antique shop window, Horncastle;
Ludford village sign; Stacked pantiles, Barton-upon-Humber

Wolds

THE WOLDS STRETCH for a distance of around 40 miles from the Humber bank in the north until the abrupt change to fenland just south of Spilsby and Horncastle. This area of chalk upland certainly disproves the notion that Lincolnshire is flat. Here there are picturesque rolling hills and sheltered valleys. Villages tend to be small and scattered and many have place names ending 'by' which shows that they were settled by Danish invaders. Two ancient routes cross the Wolds and both give splendid views; one is the Bluestone Heath Road which runs from the A157 near Welton le Wold in a south-easterly sweep to end at the A16 near Ulceby Cross. The other is the High Street which branches off from the A158 near Baumber and runs northwards to Caistor. The market towns of Horncastle, Market Rasen, Caistor, Louth, Alford and Spilsby lie at the foot of the hills.

Horncastle was once famous for its horse fair but nowadays it has become a centre of the antiques trade, while a few miles to the north is the motor racing circuit at Cadwell Park. In contrast Market Rasen is home to horse racing and it has a year-round programme of jump racing events. Louth may be tucked against the eastern edge of the Wolds but its slender church spire can be seen for miles around. Perhaps the most famous pupil at its grammar school was the poet Alfred Tennyson who had been born in the village of Somersby. At the northern end of the Wolds is the town of Barton-upon-Humber where once there were ferries that crossed to Hull but now there is the great Humber Bridge. Here also was the centre of the brick and tile industry that utilised the clay deposits found along the southern bank of the Humber.

Gunby Hall

Now in the care of the National Trust, this house was built in 1700 for the Massingberd family, and extended in the late nineteenth century. The house is full of family treasures, and there is also a stable courtyard with tearoom, and a walled garden with wonderfully fragrant roses.

Opposite: **Lincoln Red Cattle grazing at Red Hill Nature Reserve**
Known for their beautiful colour, their steady placid nature, and as good converters of forage, this traditional breed is gaining popularity with those who want locally produced, high quality beef. The cattle are grazing Lincolnshire's Coronation Meadow, one of 60 flagship meadows set up across the country as part of the celebrations of the 60th Anniversary of the Queen's coronation. In summer the meadow is a fine example of flower-rich chalk downland, alive with bees and butterflies, but cattle are introduced in the autumn after the hay crop has been taken.

Inset: **Marbled white butterfly on greater knapweed**

Left: **Louth church spire above Upgate**

The tall slim spire of St James's church is a landmark for miles around. In 1844 in the days before photography, William Brown, an enterprising Louth resident, used the scaffold that had been placed around the spire to climb to the top and make sketches of the views all around. It then took three years to transfer the sketches onto two huge canvasses which hang today in the Town Council offices, although replicas can be seen in the town's award winning museum.

Opposite: **Market day in Louth**

On Wednesdays, Fridays and Saturdays there is an extra buzz in the centre of Louth when colourful stalls fill the Market Place, drawing in shoppers and visitors from miles around. The town is justly famous for its wealth of independent shops alongside the national brands.

Sir Joseph Banks Centre, Horncastle

These recently restored buildings on Bridge Street in Horncastle commemorate one of the most famous men of Lincolnshire and one of the greatest figures of Georgian England. As a young man Joseph Banks joined the three year voyage of Captain Cook to circumnavigate the globe and explore the southern hemisphere. Along with his fellow scientists he was responsible for collecting and naming many new plants and animals. He was made President of The Royal Society and was instrumental in developing the Royal Botanic Gardens at Kew.

Horse sculpture, Horncastle

Made locally, the metal horse sculptures on Jubilee Way in Horncastle reflect the fact that the town had one of the largest horse fairs in the country during the nineteenth century. Horses were bred on the Wolds for saddle and coach, while the Lincolnshire Black, which is believed to be the progenitor of the shire-horse, came from the fens around Boston. The horses were shown in the streets, with dealers coming from this country and from overseas, most staying in the town's many inns.

Opposite: **The Town Pump, Caistor**
The name of Caistor indicates that it
was once a Roman camp so the town
has a long history. The Market Place is
surrounded by Georgian and Victorian
buildings and enhanced by the many
colourful planters. It was here that the
Town Pump was situated, topped by the
wonderful gold lion that commemorates
Queen Victoria's Diamond Jubilee
of 1897.

Right: **Statue of**
Sir John Franklin, Spilsby
Born in Spilsby in 1786, Sir John
Franklin was a Royal Navy officer
who took part in several naval battles,
undertook pioneering surveys of
Australia's coastline, served as governor
of Tasmania, and searched the icy waters
of northern Canada for the elusive
North-West Passage. He was never
to return from his final voyage as his
ships became ice-locked and eventually
all the crews perished.

Mud and stud cottage, Thimbleby

Humble cottages constructed of mud and stud were once widespread in the county, but many have been demolished. The village of Thimbleby is fortunate in retaining some picturesque examples of this form of construction, the walls being made from a mud mix plastered over a rough wooden framework, topped by low thatched roofs.

Opposite: **Old Bolingbroke Castle**

In the Middle Ages Bolingbroke was an important market town and the Castle belonged to the Duchy of Lancaster. First built in the thirteenth century, the Castle had a curtain wall with five horseshoe towers and a double-towered gatehouse, encircled by a wide moat. It became one of the homes of John of Gaunt and his son, later Henry IV, was born there in 1367.

Motor bikers at Willingham Woods

There is a car park and picnic site at Willingham Woods for those who want to walk in the pinewoods, while the café is particularly busy at weekends and in the summer as it is a popular stopping-off point for motorists, cyclists and particularly motor bikers who break their journeys to and from the coast.

Walking in Hubbard's Hills, Louth
This beautiful wooded valley with its chalk stream was bought for the people of Louth in 1907 with money left in the will of Auguste Pahud, in memory of his wife Annie who came from nearby Withern. Now run as a charity, the site is visited by thousands of people every year.

Coast

THE LINCOLNSHIRE COAST stretches from the Humber to the Wash and it is backed by the Outmarsh, a land of rich grazing pasture divided by narrow dykes. Grimsby is the largest town and it is famous for its fishing heritage. The true seaside towns are Cleethorpes, Mablethorpe and Skegness; once small fishing villages these towns expanded rapidly when the railways arrived to bring in crowds of people anxious to sample the bracing fresh air and enjoy the fun of a seaside holiday. Other parts of the coast are protected as nature reserves with their sand dunes, salt and freshwater marsh, sand and mud flats, all managed for their unique wildlife, notably the breeding colony of grey seals at Donna Nook, and the migrant birds which arrive and depart each spring and autumn.

Seaside buckets and spades; The Jolly Fisherman, Skegness; Sea buckthorn berries

Opposite: Sandy beach at Crook Bank, near Mablethorpe

Grey seals at Donna Nook
From late October to the end of December grey seals come ashore onto the sands and mudflats of the Donna Nook National Nature Reserve to give birth, a spectacle that attracts large numbers of visitors from across the country. The pups are born with white coats and they suckle from their mothers for about three weeks before they are abandoned. The pups then shed their white coats and hunger eventually drives them out to sea to search for food.

Left: **Saltfleetby-Theddlethorpe Dunes National Nature Reserve**
This nature reserve is internationally important for its range of coastal habitats including mudflats, sand dunes, salt and freshwater marsh. In summer the established dunes support a rich flora including pyramidal and bee orchids, with abundant butterflies, while the freshwater marsh maintains water voles and many species of dragonfly. The salt marsh looks spectacular in midsummer when the sea lavender is flowering.

Funfair at Cleethorpes

Once a small fishing hamlet, Cleethorpes first became popular for sea bathing in the late eighteenth century. But it was the arrival of the railway in 1863 that really accelerated the development of this popular seaside resort.

Cleethorpes Pier

The pier was opened in 1873 and was originally much longer, but it was shortened during the Second World War to prevent it being used in a German invasion attempt. The Pavilion has a tearoom, bar and restaurant, and a recently restored multifunctional space for conferences and weddings.

Motor bikes racing at Mablethorpe
During the winter months there are regular motor cycle sand racing events held at Mablethorpe. The combination of speed and noise appeals to those who enjoy extreme action sports.

Opposite: **Donkey rides at Mablethorpe**
During the summer months young children enjoy the unhurried pace of the donkeys that give rides on the sandy beach.

Covenham Reservoir

The reservoir was constructed in the 1960s to meet the demand for drinking water from Grimsby and Cleethorpes. It is up to twenty metres deep and the path around the circumference is 2 miles long. Part of the reservoir is a nature reserve but there is also a watersports centre offering sailing, windsurfing, waterskiing and diving.

Opposite: **Waves on the beach**

Lincolnshire's Natural Coast is one of its best kept secrets. Visitors can enjoy the sounds of the waves and the birds along miles of unspoilt sandy beach.

Opposite: **National Fishing Heritage Centre, Grimsby**
The Heritage Centre at Alexandra Dock allows visitors to experience the sights, sounds and smells of life on a fishing trawler in the 1950s. Tours are also available of the *Ross Tiger* moored alongside. This trawler fished the North Sea for twenty-seven years from 1957 to 1984.

Right: **The Fishermen's Memorial, Grimsby**
In St James's Square and close to the Minster is the memorial to the fishermen from Grimsby who went to sea but failed to return. Created by public donation it was dedicated in 2005. The sculptor Trevor Harries has captured the difficult conditions in which the fishermen worked.

All Saints church, Saltfleetby
The names of Saltfleet and Saltfleetby (Sollerby to the locals) show that long ago salt production was an important industry in the area. After high tides the salt-rich silt from the upper shore was scooped up, placed in a trough and water poured onto it to produce a brine solution which was then boiled to crystallise the salt. The medieval church of All Saints has a tower that leans outwards but nevertheless seems quite sturdy.

Cattle grazing on the marshes
The importance of the coastal grazing marshes has been recently recognised by a project involving local communities in the protection of these habitats. Seasonally wet grassland and surrounding ditches are an important habitat for breeding waders and wintering wildfowl.

Fens

THE FLAT LANDSCAPE and big skies of the Fens have their own special appeal. Here the rivers have been straightened and many new dykes have been dug, all with the purpose of getting water off the land. But the resulting soils are some of the most productive in the country so that alongside great fields of wheat and oilseed rape, are vast expanses of potatoes and green vegetable crops. Daffodil bulbs are grown, early crops are encouraged under polythene, and there are some huge glasshouses. Boston, once second only to London in importance as a port, is still the largest town, and its magnificent church tower, known as

'The Stump' is a landmark for miles around. Many of the older settlements like Holbeach and Long Sutton are found along the slightly higher silt bank that separates the land on the seaward side that has been reclaimed from the sea, from the drained peat soils on the landward side. Spalding was once the centre of the bulb-growing industry but now draws visitors to its Springfields shopping outlet. Crowland was another town that was once an island in the marshy wilderness; it grew up around the monastery with its shrine to St Guthlac.

Cabbages; Pumpkins; Daffodils

Opposite: View across East Fen

Sibsey Trader Mill

Built in 1877 to replace an earlier wooden post mill, this windmill has a tall, slender tower which can be seen for miles around in the flat landscape of West Fen. Described as the best-looking windmill in the county, it took its name from the nearby Lincoln Trader Inn which is now demolished. It is one of the few six-sailed windmills remaining in England, and can be visited throughout the summer months.

Fosdyke Yacht Haven

A marina has been established on the tidal River Welland at Fosdyke Bridge offering a range of facilities to boat owners. The River Welland rises in Northamptonshire but flows through Stamford and Spalding, crossing the South Holland fens, before reaching The Wash.

Left: **The Stump overlooking
The Haven, the tidal section
of the River Witham**
St Botolph's has been described as
a giant among parish churches
which reflects the former
importance of the town and port
of Boston. In its heyday the
town was second only to London,
and it was the wealth of its local
merchants that funded such a fine
building with its towering
steeple.

Opposite: **Crowland Abbey**
The abbey was founded many
centuries ago on an island in the
fen. The present parish church
occupies part of the original
abbey church, and the churchyard
is crowded with gravestones,
many from the seventeenth,
eighteenth and early nineteenth
centuries with fine examples of
stone carving, lettering and
decoration.

View of Boston from St Botolph's church tower, looking north-east

The stone building in the left foreground is the old Sessions House built in 1841-43, and alongside is the County Hall built in 1825-27, which now houses the library on the ground floor. The Centenary Methodist Chapel is in the left middle distance with Central Park behind. Maud Foster windmill is in the background and the blue building on the horizon is Pilgrim Hospital.

View of Boston from St Botolph's church tower, looking east

The statue of Herbert Ingram, the founder of *The Illustrated London News*, is in the foreground with the Market Place and shops beyond. The four-storey neo-Gothic building in the row of shops was, for over one hundred years, the department store of Small & Co. The yellow-brick building in the right foreground is Lloyds Bank, formerly Garfit & Claypon's Bank, and the stone building just beyond the church in the left foreground is Barclays Bank, originally the Boston, Stamford & Spalding Bank. The football ground of Boston United FC is visible in the right distance.

Frampton Marsh Nature Reserve

This coastal wetland nature reserve, managed by the Royal Society for the Protection of Birds, has freshwater scrapes, areas of reedbed and wet grassland, all created to bring the wildlife of the Wash closer to the visiting public who can explore the footpaths and use the viewing hides. In the summer there are breeding lapwing, redshank and avocet, while in the winter large flocks of brent geese graze on the fields.

Opposite: **Salt marsh at Holbeach St Matthew**

The Wash is a vast estuary that stretches from Skegness on the Lincolnshire coast round to Hunstanton in Norfolk. The intertidal banks of sand and mud gradually merge into areas of salt marsh dissected by tidal creeks. Although seemingly bleak and uninviting in appearance, these open spaces support a wealth of wildlife.

Springfields Outlet Shopping and Festival Gardens, Spalding
Springfields offers a blend of over fifty outlet stores, including many well-known high street brands, with 25 acres of beautiful gardens and leisure attractions. During the summer months a water taxi operates along the River Welland, linking the outlet to the town centre.

Daffodil fields near Moulton Seas End
Daffodils have replaced the once numerous fields of tulips that were a feature in the Fens. Grown for their flowers and their bulbs, they provide a welcome springtime splash of colour.

Trinity Bridge, Crowland

This unique bridge with its three arches once spanned the confluence of the River Welland and a tributary and the River Witham. All these water courses have now been re-routed so that the bridge stands on dry land. The three sets of steps converge at the top and there is a well-worn statue, possibly of Christ, that is thought to have come from the front of Crowland Abbey.

Market Hill Mosaic, Holbeach

Elements of the history of this Fenland market town are celebrated in the mosaic in the town centre. The river and its wildlife, land reclamation and farming, and the granting of a market charter, are depicted alongside local famous faces from the twentieth century.

Vales

THE VALES HAS AN undulating landscape with attractive villages built of the local mellow limestone. There are also some fine country houses, like Belton House in its spacious park on the outskirts of Grantham, and Grimsthorpe Castle between Bourne and Corby Glen. Sir Isaac Newton was born at Woolsthorpe and he is celebrated there and in Grantham where he attended the grammar school. Woodlands are particular features of the area, and one of the oldest and largest oak trees in the country is found near Bourne. The A1, or the Great North Road to give it its more romantic name, skirts the western edge of Lincolnshire. Once it passed through Stamford and Grantham and there are many present-day hotels in these towns that date back to the hostelries and coaching inns that were dotted along this important route, offering food and accommodation to travellers, and a change of horses for their carriages.

Clock tower at Belton House; Plaque on Woolsthorpe Manor; Topiary peacock at Grimsthorpe Castle

Opposite: View in Stamford

Belton House

Belton House was built for the Brownlow family and each generation has left its mark in the house, formal gardens and deer park. It has been described as the perfect English country house and is now in the care of the National Trust. The stable yard houses a café, restaurant, and shops selling gifts, garden products and second-hand books, while the park plays host to a range of open air events throughout the year.

South front, Belton House

The first stone of the house was laid in 1685 but nearly a century later it was given a face-lift by James Wyatt. The south front is a glorious mix of steps, balustrades, urns and niches, the golden Ancaster stone glowing in the sunlight.

Woolsthorpe Manor

This manor house of the seventeenth century was the birthplace of Sir Isaac Newton in 1642. Reputedly, Isaac was sitting in the orchard when an apple fell from one of the trees and this inspired his thoughts on gravity. The house is a National Trust property and there is also a hands-on Science Discovery Centre and coffee shop.

Opposite, left: **Isaac's Apple sculpture, Wyndham Park, Grantham**

Carved from the trunk of a horse-chestnut tree that grew on the site, this sculpture of a hand forms the centrepiece to the Sensory Garden in Wyndham Park. The apple is carved from elm and the design picks up the story of Isaac Newton.

Opposite, right: **Statue of Sir Isaac Newton, St Peter's Hill, Grantham**

The celebrated English physicist and mathematician is remembered in Grantham by this statue of 1858, placed near to the Town Hall, which now has a new lease of life as the Guildhall Arts Centre. The statue is said to have been cast from the metal of a Russian gun captured during the Crimean War.

St Paul's Street, Stamford
This street in the centre of Stamford has a wonderful mix of old buildings with their roofs of Collyweston stone slates. These are not proper slates but a limestone quarried at Collyweston, just over the county boundary in Northamptonshire, which splits easily to form this traditional roofing material.

Grimsthorpe Castle, north front

Not really a castle, this is the magnificent home of the Earls of Ancaster. Set in parkland landscaped by Capability Brown, the house is approached down a long avenue. In the early eighteenth century the north front was rebuilt to designs by Sir John Vanbrugh.

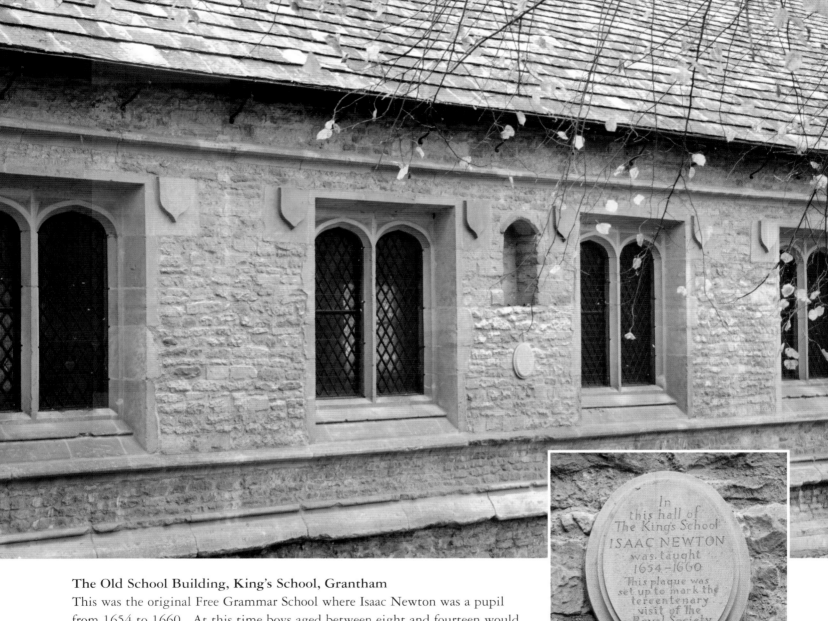

The Old School Building, King's School, Grantham

This was the original Free Grammar School where Isaac Newton was a pupil from 1654 to 1660. At this time boys aged between eight and fourteen would have been taught Latin and Greek. The plaque commemorates a visit by members of The Royal Society in 1960, three hundred years after its formation.

Maiden Lane, Stamford

Stamford claims to be the finest stone town in England. With its wealth of surviving seventeenth and eighteenth century buildings the streetscape has featured in many costume dramas, and it is regarded as one of the best places to live in Britain.

Grimsthorpe Castle, south front

The south front of Grimsthorpe Castle retains much of its original Tudor appearance, the house being originally built for Charles Brandon, Duke of Suffolk and close ally of Henry VIII. There are attractive formal and topiary gardens which lead into the wilder woodland garden.

Opposite: **Bowthorpe Oak, Manthorpe, near Bourne**

This giant oak tree is reputed to be over one thousand years old. The gnarled and hollow trunk has in the past been used by children to play inside and hold parties, but there are now chains to prevent it from splitting under the weight of its heavy boughs.

Blue Pig pub sign, Grantham

In the nineteenth century there were several 'blue' public houses in Grantham, the colour showing that they belonged to the Manners family from nearby Belvoir Castle, and supported the political party known as the Whigs. There was great rivalry at this time with the Brownlow family from Belton House to control the borough.

The Angel and Royal, Grantham

There has been an inn on this site for hundreds of years, as it stood on the Great North Road, the main route from London to Edinburgh. There have been many royal visitors to the inn over the centuries but the old Angel Inn did not become the Angel and Royal until 1866 to commemorate a visit by Edward, Prince of Wales and heir to the throne.

Countryside South

THIS AREA HAS the southern section of the limestone heath running through the centre, with the cliff-edge villages looking west over the Trent Vale through which the Rivers Witham and Brant flow. To the east there is a strip of fenland and then a ridge of slightly higher ground, the latter much wooded around Bardney, but changing to sandy heathland around Woodhall Spa. Sleaford is the main market town and here many of the important buildings have been built with the local Ancaster limestone. Woodhall Spa was a village until the mid nineteenth century when spa water was discovered and it became a resort. It still retains its quaint Edwardian character and now hosts the National Golf Centre. Close by are the neighbouring villages of Tattershall and Coningsby. Tattershall has the finest brick castle keep in the country while the Battle of Britain Memorial Flight is housed at RAF Coningsby. During the Second World War there were forty-nine airfields spread over Lincolnshire and it became known as 'Bomber County', so it seems very apt that the only remaining airworthy Avro Lancaster is based here. A second Lancaster known as 'Just Jane' is held by the Lincolnshire Aviation Heritage Centre at East Kirkby and this gives taxi-rides on the old runway.

Sign for the Battle of Britain Memorial Flight, RAF Coningsby; Close up of 'Thumper', PA474 Avro Lancaster, RAF Coningsby; RAF 617 Squadron Memorial, Woodhall Spa

Opposite: View over Potterhanworth Fen towards Bardney

The Broadway, Woodhall Spa
In late Victorian and Edwardian times Woodhall developed into a spa town after healing waters were found. The tree-lined Broadway with its arcade of shops was laid out at that time.

The Kinema in the Woods, Woodhall Spa
The Kinema began as a meeting room and tennis and cricket pavilion but when the popularity of the town began to decline in the 1920s it was re-developed into a picture house. At that time the best seats were deck chairs at the front, while there were benches at the back for those who wanted the cheaper seats. This cinema is unique in having back projection and it continues to thrive.

Washing 'Thumper', PA474 Avro Lancaster, RAF Coningsby
RAF Coningsby is home to the Battle of Britain Memorial Flight, a fleet of historic aircraft, with pride of place going to its Avro Lancaster bomber. These majestic aeroplanes played a crucial role in the Second World War, and although over seven thousand were built, this is the only one still flying in this country. Throughout the summer months the Lancaster, together with a Dakota, Spitfires and Hurricanes, takes part in flying displays up and down the country, but at the end of the season the aeroplane is given a thorough clean before it goes into the hangar for its winter overhaul. The Lancaster proudly displays the coat of arms of the City of Lincoln and it is currently painted to represent 'Thumper Mk III' with the code letters 'KC-A', a Lancaster which flew with the famous 617 Squadron after the Dambusters raid in 1943.

The Petwood Hotel, Woodhall Spa
Built as a private house in the first decade of the twentieth century, the Petwood Hotel was requisitioned by the RAF during the Second World War and it served as the Officers Mess for 617 Squadron. Today the Squadron Bar displays memorabilia and tributes to some of those officers, and it proudly flies the Royal Air Force Ensign.

Tattershall Castle

Built by Ralph Cromwell, Lord High Treasurer of England during the reign of Henry VI, the brick tower keep is as impressive today as it was five hundred and eighty years ago. The use of brick as a building material was still quite unusual at that time and it has been estimated that around seven hundred thousand were required. The castle was saved from destruction by Lord Curzon of Kedleston who restored it and passed it to the National Trust in 1925.

Opposite: **The former Greyhound Inn, Folkingham**

The former coaching inn dominates the picturesque village green. Its heyday was in the eighteenth and early nineteenth centuries when coaches would have stopped here regularly for a change of horses and refreshment for the passengers on their journeys between Lincoln and London. There was also an assembly room used for social gatherings and this is where the Quarter Session courts were held.

Bardney Limewoods National Nature Reserve

The nature reserve is a collection of small woodlands near Bardney where the native small-leaved lime occurs. They have been high forest or managed as coppice since at least the eleventh century. In spring the ground flora is particularly attractive and then in the autumn there is another burst of colour before the leaves fall. Several of the woods are owned and managed by the Forestry Commission and are open to the public.

Opposite: Kirkby Moor Nature Reserve

This nature reserve, managed by the Lincolnshire Wildlife Trust, is a remnant of the once extensive heathlands that are found in the Woodhall district. In late August when the heather is in flower the reserve is a wonderful sight.

Opposite: **Site of Bardney Abbey**

In the Middle Ages several monasteries were founded along the valley of the River Witham; the river being an important trade link between Lincoln and Boston. The sites included Bardney, Barlings and Tupholme, but they were all closed down by the hand of Henry VIII. Since that time much of the building stone has been robbed so that little remains above ground, but at Bardney the 'lumps and bumps' in the ground reveal the layout of the former abbey, while some of the excavated carved stone is displayed in the village church.

Right: **Heckington windmill**

This eight-sailed windmill is believed to be the only complete example of this type in the country. The windmill tower was built in 1830 and originally it was fitted with five sails. The eight sails, which came from a windmill in Boston, were first fitted to the windmill in 1892. There have since been further repairs and restorations, the last in 2014 when a large crane was used to hoist eight new sails into place, so that flour milling can once again take place, weather permitting.

The National Centre for Craft & Design, Sleaford
The historic market town of Sleaford grew up at a crossing of the River Slea, and there was a 'New' and 'Old' town. In a converted seed warehouse on one of the old wharves in the centre of the town, this modern arts centre comprises exhibition space, design workshops, a shop and café. It also offers a year-round, all-age learning and events programme.